33 OFFERINGS

Daniel Richmond

This book is dedicated to the freedom of Truth
and the beauty of Love.

All net proceeds generated from the sale
of this book are donated to charitable causes.

TABLE OF CONTENTS

The Love 55

About the Author 81

About the Mandalas 85

33 Offerings

THE PRAYER

The longing for Truth,
is a runaway train,
that cuts through all fear,
all wind, fire and rain.

Questions

How can gain,
undo pain,
if we never,
let it drain?

Why is fear,
often near,
of the things,
we hold so dear?

What is loss,
in life's toss,
if we carry,
our own cross?

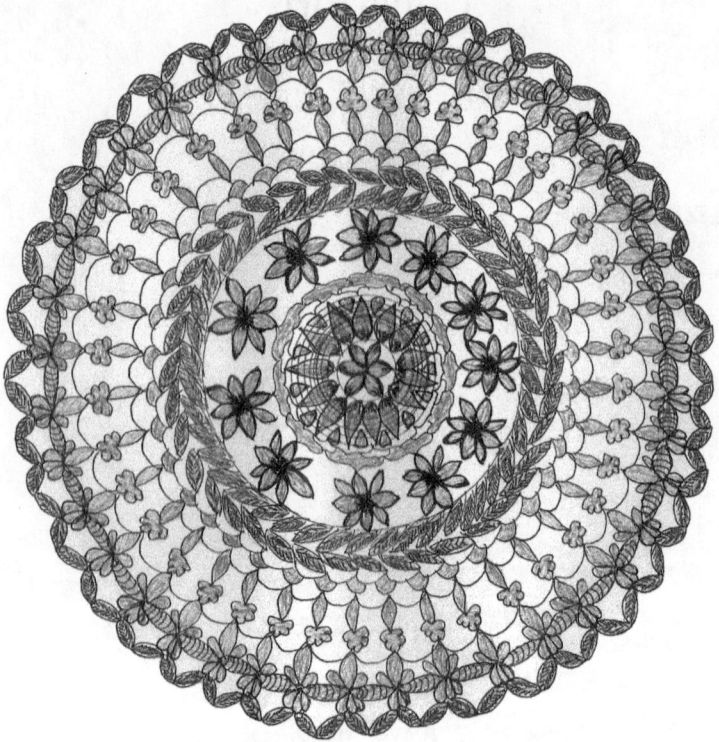

Searching

Where have we placed our goal?
where did we leave our dreams?
we keep looking through the soul,
for the Truth our heart deems.

We wrap ourselves in words,
a blanket of quilted thought,
that disguise the world that is,
and the lessons that we're taught.

And again we find that goal,
as we gasp for one last breath,
overcoming fear and doubt,
of our dreams in life and death.

The Veil

Transparent is the cloak of concern,
which covers the Self so closely,
and taints our ability to discern,
fear from Love, Divine from worldly.

This curtain we carry, this trap we devise,
our relative truth, our own little world,
sees absolute oneness smile in disguise,
yet keeps our heart so gripped and curled.

Awareness of being can cure this ill,
as pure constant longing shows us the way,
the courage of lions that feed on our will,
can clear the visions our veils portray.

Mind

Many lifetimes can be spent,
getting this machine to feel,
making concepts out of fears,
to relate with what seems real.

Through the eyeglass of mind,
realities can be friend or foe,
our emotions intertwined,
upon judgments we bestow.

In the deepest of our being,
intuition holds the key,
and the answers we all seek,
which our minds will never see.

Arrogance

What a fool is one who believes,
that there are none wiser than he,
through arrogance his heart bleeds,
and caught in pride's denial he be.

Is anything gained in separation?
If all that lives communes with life,
he who rejects in desperation,
is held hostage by his own knife.

Remove those clouds that shield,
an untrue sense of inferiority,
and let yourself open and yield,
to greater lessons in humility.

Fear

It comes to please me at times,
seducing me through its many ways,
holding my hand as I fall asleep,
and swiftly numbing these passing days.

Distracting myself with a trick or two,
I fail to see this magician's hand,
illusion becomes the brother of Truth,
and not even I know where I stand.

Fear old friend, you know me so well,
better than I will ever know you,
but beware of Love whom once you've met,
discerning our fears from all that is True.

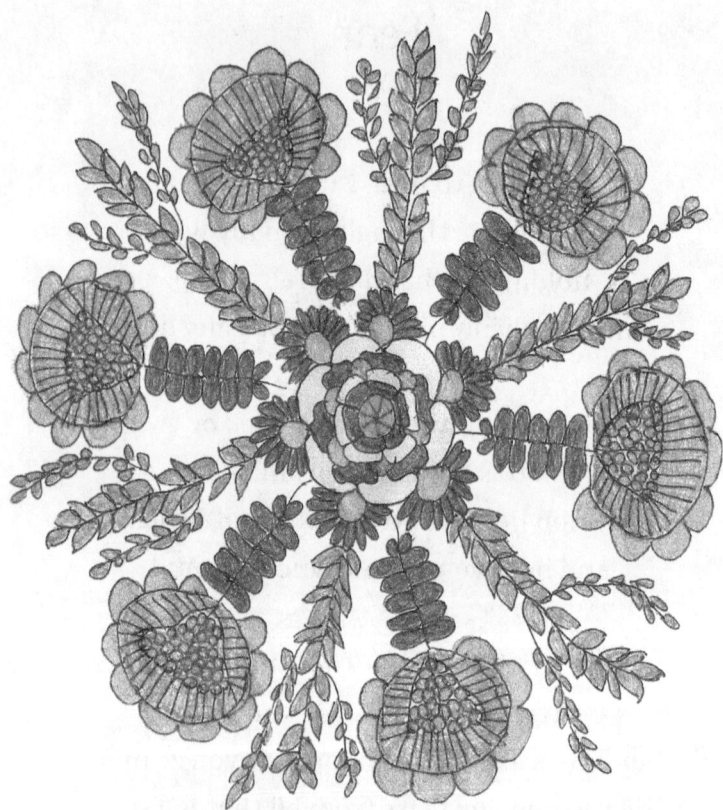

The Child

A child resides in every man's mind,
keeping the growth from shining through,
it dreams, it doubts, it lives and dies,
as mirrors reflect on each other's view.

He often falls from branch to branch,
and swings from mood to mood,
this tree of life he continues to climb,
to reach what shall be understood.

On his shoulders the burden of time,
deep in his heart the light of Truth,
in his veins the freedom of Love,
as timeless wisdom matures his youth.

Choices

In the tempting allure,
of narrowing stances,
and by doubting ourselves,
should or shouldn't arises.

So we go in that circle,
that bubble of concern,
never knowing to reach,
to believe, try and learn.

There's a cure so simple,
in our personal stake,
to the questions of self,
and the choices we make.

Desire

Desire tip toed its way into this blazing cave,
where a nest of sleepless fantasies laid,
it spoke rolling its tongue in a seductive way,
sharing a blurred vision so clearly displayed.

Out of emptiness' own desperate measure,
it showed me what I needed to see,
created a list of things I should treasure,
as it whispered in my ear 'who I wanted to be'.

I stayed so unconscious and eagerly numb,
believing these tales of pleasure and gain,
as life passed me by to the beat of a drum,
that sees not the Truth and avoids further pain.

Buenos Aires

Intimacy with Truth and inspiration,
led me to the center of the fire,
and in the deepest roots of self,
faced the flames of burning desire.

In the beauty of tango and wine,
ghosts and shadows enter the night,
feelings up and down my spine,
which are often needless to fight.

By day the goodness of clean air,
light uncovers all darkness within,
still in this city a scent of despair,
dried tears, passion, love and sin.

Sin

Sin is falling short of sin-cerity,
to one's self and one's aspiration,
it is giving up on our true calling,
on the search for Love's liberation.

A delusion rooted in guilt,
often feeding self aggression,
but nonetheless it's a lesson,
a gift to unwrap with compassion.

Who can truly define betrayal?
or the purest measure of sanity?
if it is found within ourselves,
the place wherein lies all clarity.

THE RESPONSE

Ask me if I am falling in Love,
I shall answer from the ground,
Listen for the doubt in my heart,
And you will not hear a sound.

Feel and See

In every moment,
feel eternity,
in every life,
see Divinity.

In every space,
feel completeness,
in every piece,
see the wholeness.

In every heartbeat,
feel the Love,
in every one,
see one God.

Divinity

In the presence of Grace,
all falls away,
the sour becomes sweet,
and sweetness turns to Love.

At the feet of Truth,
desire loses grasp,
the emptiness becomes Whole,
and Wholeness leads our life.

Through the eyes of the Divine,
all is seen,
darkness infused with light,
as lightning strikes our hearts.

Sincerity

As sincerity knocks on your door,
so shall your heart heed the call,
the will kneels at the feet of courage,
and rises in mid-air as all worries fall.

Yet those who still remain timid,
or dismiss God's play on the soul,
in this virtuous mountain of life,
would do best to rethink their goal.

Taste this nectar of surrender,
there is no intense sweetness alike,
dive from the furthest of stars,
and embrace the thrill of this hike.

The Friend

As a tidal wave emerging in eternity,
like an infinite army of wild horses,
She awaits the signal of our heart's unity,
with Self, the world and all its forces.

The Friend becomes known to us,
graciously declaring freedom for all,
in the depths of such Divine silence,
with an omniscience that is unmistakable.

The battle begins and ends all at once,
joy, grief, laughter, weeps and wails,
through every doorway She passes,
as ecstasy fills the air and heaven unveils.

Self Deception

A new seductive illusion is fetched,
for a heart that is willingly torn,
as love continues to be stretched,
and remains sleepless and unborn.

Another dream to awaken from,
a thousand losses disguised by gain,
and one addiction to which I succumb,
those exquisite memories of pain.

My never ending means to an end,
in a life veiled by my own perception,
and hidden desires I long to transcend,
by a force greater than self deception.

Devotion

Such peace in devotion,
such strength comes alive,
in kneeling to Truth,
does freedom abide.

A life filled with longing,
awakens great joy,
from humble beginnings,
will God's grace deploy.

Our days without sorrow,
with Love ever more,
the sun's blissful morrow,
through every heart's door.

Words

Words may often cut like swords,
where Truth and falsity transpose,
and in the spring when lovers meet,
they are like the petals of a rose.

But Love that feeds the hungry soul,
needs not a single word expressed,
nor written verse or gallant prose,
to let the feeble heart be blessed.

Its words that were not spoken yet,
what all our cravings long to hear,
before our troubled minds forget,
those memories we hold so dear.

The Lotus

In muddy waters we utter our first desires,
the fragile seeds of life begin to open up,
a deep wisdom that guides and inspires,
feeds and nourishes as we empty our cup.

Though memories often blur what we see,
and convictions keep pushing peace away,
the lotus of our hearts is still wild and free,
sees no fear nor abides in our dismay.

Love abound we head back to the source,
as the beauty of life continues to spring,
we flourish outwardly by an internal force,
with no restrictions our soul begins to sing.

Wisdom

On whom or what can one rely?
when such ignorance lurks about,
and the arrogance of pride,
keeps us wavering in doubt.

Where is knowledge and its source?
and its roots of endless reach,
that can cure the ills of world,
and the blinding thoughts we preach.

The sacred union of Love,
is the wisdom of life's stages,
often speechless even wordless,
simply carried through the ages.

In the Rain

Have you ever secretly wept for Love?
or ached in the shadows of beauty,
while the soul was flying high above,
carrying the burden of seeming duty.

In the sweet depths of a humble heart,
where the silence explains all things,
a Truth revealed tears your world apart,
and from deep within new life begins.

Feeling what once seemed distant and far,
Free at last from all sorrows and pain,
Beauty and Love define all that you are,
the artist, the canvas, the flower in the rain.

Separation

They say let God in,
they say live and learn,
I say let God out,
I say Love and yearn.

Running east,
while pointing west,
where the sun shines,
and the souls rest.

Illusion of separation,
between that and this,
just be still and feel,
where the Freedom is.

THE LOVE

Oh Divine Love in me,
would Freedom be here,
if You would not be,
if You were not near.

The Path

A world of comfort,
a world of pain,
the peace in loss,
the gain in vain.

A light within,
a dark tomorrow,
a day in joy,
a day in sorrow.

The search of Self,
as self derails,
the end of fear,
as Love prevails.

Moments

Upon the thoughts of who we are,
this life changes in so many ways,
we look within and search without,
as moments pass and so do days.

Felt the pleasures and the pains,
time stood still, then seemed lost,
for an instant freedom reigned,
till fear was induced by its cost.

Now the spaces open widely,
to embrace what is still unknown,
and we gather our own selves,
as our eager hearts atone.

Dreams

Beneath our wings rest our dreams,
and in our dreams the heart takes flight,
above this play, holding our view,
as deep within we gather might.

And so we wake from this long sleep,
learning to see with dreamers' eyes,
things that were, no longer seem,
no longer fooled by their disguise.

Dreams and play are words of fools,
some hardened soul may say to you,
and doubt will surely come our way,
to test the strength of fortune's few.

Honesty

We water Truth within ourselves,
in being truthful towards another,
our hearts are freed by letting go,
of masks we use to run for cover.

As what we yearn for deep inside,
becomes the force of all we do,
the need to shield or self protect,
is placed aside with what's untrue.

A deep respect and Love of self,
dissolves all guilt and doubtful voices,
the selfless nature we truly are,
in pure heart will lead our choices.

Just Be

We gather, collect, protect and so we fill our minds,
as we seek and search we build brick upon brick,
on a basis of innocent ignorance that thrives,
and neglects to see impatience's own trick.

If we fall, we rise up as quick as we can,
to form our fearful selves once again,
we refine and fine tune and perfect,
to make sure a self will remain.

The secret is surrender,
silence the key,
emptiness,
just be.

Humility

With the strength of a lion,
on our knees like a child,
we return to our center,
when desires run wild.

And if pride keeps us high,
caught in fears of sin,
let us open our eyes,
to compassion within.

There is no wrong or right,
as we travel this maze,
there is only the light,
and its humbling ways.

Light

Feel and harbor the light within,
your heart be a prism of awareness Divine,
firm in the wind, light does not flinch,
nor does it tremble, retract or resign.

Connect even deeper to the wholeness of life,
the giver, the presence, the mother of all,
merging, embracing, completeness alive!
returning back home as illusions fall.

Here in this place surrender the self,
detaching the soul from body and mind,
all that remains is once again light,
so willing to Love, so present, so kind.

Awakening

In the arms of Love I slept,
and my dreams were transformed,
all doubt in the heart had been swept,
and revived all the feelings I once mourned.

Warm kindness I breathed in the night,
as the airs of true triumph arrived,
through a torch that burns blissfully bright,
and is source of all life here derived.

So what more can we do in this life?
than bring Love where there is hate,
and sweet joy where there is strife,
for the good of humanity's fate.

Whispers

Have you heard with eyes closed?
the murmurs in the forest below,
or whispers in the mountain top,
long resonating since ages ago.

Eternal sounds of the invisible,
of which our hearts truly speak,
as this life unfolds its miracle,
revealing the peace we seek.

We are all but naked feathers,
in the winds of a universal will,
a world seems to move and shake,
yet we are silent, blissful and still.

Untitled

A poem begins titled as Love,
the lines are born out of such,
words slowly finding themselves,
poured with a delicate touch.

Lights of Truth clear the way,
as compassion leads this quest,
in the midst of troubled rhymes,
patient kindness do all but rest.

Pen stops and title is changed,
the end becomes the start,
and the question still remains,
"what is Love?" says this heart.

Love

Love is quite hard to describe,
or define in actions and deeds,
very often dressed as compassion,
engaging life and all our needs.

It's silence beneath kind words,
sheer strength when all is lost,
the joy beyond time and space,
how we surrender above all cost.

ever present in all our hearts,
where ourselves we truly discover,
a beginning, middle and the end,
yearning of itself from one another.

ABOUT THE AUTHOR

Daniel Richmond's poetry vividly portrays the author's own search for the purest of all - in Love and in Truth. With the earnestness of the uninitiated, he shares in gritty detail his journey towards deeper discernment and Ultimate Truth. He celebrates the vistas of insight and revelation as well as the darker moments of test and trial throughout his journey, discovering along the way every aspect: from pitfalls to magic, from naiveté to true innocence, from sensual to essential.

From the heart of great adventure and an insatiable hunger for the deepest wisdom, Daniel's poetry is both unsettling and uplifting. His uncompromising quest for Truth and indelible courage to face what is false, endear him to fellow travelers on the path of Self-discovery, Illumination and Love. His writing is paradoxically beautiful in its simplicity and depth, its fearlessness and trepidation, and its humility and self-assured poise. Daniel offers in his poetry a gift of tremendous sincerity, honesty, and love. He invites the reader to walk, rejoice and join this great quest.

ABOUT THE MANDALAS

After spending half a lifetime in the world of business, I discovered, by surprise and as a spontaneous act, that an outlet for my creativity is drawing Mandalas. This inspiration flowed through my commitment to grow in consciousness and to learn each and every day how to be connected with the higher Self. I later learned more about what a Mandala represents and how it can be a visual tool that helps one to enter into a deeper meditative state. Indeed I was pleasantly surprised to see how my intention to connect with the Higher Consciousness, as the Source, manifested as these drawings expressing through my creativity. They are an offering of love and a wordless companion to Daniel's vivid and stimulating poetry.

Rosa Sugrañes
December 2015
Key Biscayne, FL, USA

To read more of
Daniel Richmond's
latest work visit

www.danielrichmond.com

* 9 7 8 0 9 8 6 0 4 5 4 9 3 *